Just Keep On Doing What You're Doing

poems by Marc Pietrzykowski

for Ashley, always

Contents

Barn's burnt, now I can see the moon. — Mizuta Masahide

Upstairs, Downstairs, In-Between

The song my neighbor plays
when he comes home: unlocking
the door, turning the knob,
the stairs' squeak and clunk,
the door clicking shut behind him,
is not the song that ends
with lovers reconciled, hand
in hand, or new love unfurling
like a quilt stitched from the glances
of other lovers, half-whispered
vows, and every kind of petal.
It's not his fault. Our age
cannot bear such songs,
not because we've heard them all
before, but because we never
heard them in the first place,
we only learned them third hand
as they fell from the lips of clowns
and tyrants, the better to forget
there is no difference between the two.

Through the floor I hear his toaster
or microwave offer its siren call,
hear his footsteps across the ceiling,
imagine I can hear him sinking
into the couch. I try to love him
up through the floor, massage
his jaw gently as he chews
too fast, swallows too hard, wishing
it would just go down so he could,

for a moment, before sleep comes,
stop working. I try to tell him:
it will stop, someday, your wish
is not a wish if it is inevitable.

I would climb the stairs and make
them squeak each the same,
knock on his door, ask if he wanted
a cup of tea, but we are neighbors,
and our floors and walls and ceilings
are precious, they allow us
to sing whatever song we want,
just not so loud as to bother the others
and let them know what fools we are,
full of the same melodies we learned
when first we found our bodies
were formed for joy and wonder.

Someone Has to Steer

Through smoke rising white in the gray sky
a tug drags an empty garbage barge up a black river.

The captain burns his tongue on his coffee,
curses at the hovering gulls,
     remembers his father in the doorway
     smelling of the foundry
     arms full of Christmas presents.

He blasts the horn going under the bridge,
feels the echo in his teeth
as rain starts to tick against the windshield.

The wipers jerk and squeak.

He peels the plastic from a ham sandwich,
the same sandwich he ate yesterday,
the same he will eat tomorrow. It wiggles
     in his hand, suddenly strange
     like a snake or ticking bomb,
or a sandwich.
It's only a sandwich.

His wife made it standing at the kitchen counter,
in her scrubs, worrying they had no one
to look after them when they were old.

Mustard. Brown bread.
The sun crashes through the windshield.

He tosses the crust to the gulls,
kisses his fingertips,
presses them to his wife's photo.

They drop the barge, start a drag
on a full load. The wind is blowing down river.

Moebius

My neighbor plays thumb-piano on his porch while it snows
fat flakes, falling more or less straight down.
In the Spring, if we are all still alive, I'll watch him
plant peppers and tomatoes in his front yard
and curse at the squirrels who have learned to love both.

He drinks too much, and says ugly things to his wife,
but not often, and less than before, and their love
is a stained glass window the sun shines through
as they walk along, to the library, or ice cream shop.
He works somewhere, comes home looking tired.

When the snow slackens, he goes upstairs and sits,
his back to the window, a computer glowing on his lap,
and he types. I get the binoculars and peek at the screen:
My neighbor plays thumb-piano on his porch while it snows
fat flakes, falling more or less straight down.

Climbing the South Slope
— for Richard

Arriving late to the party, my friend and I
peck at the carcass, make jungle juice
from the dregs. The kids are upstairs
submerged in the glow of ten thousand screens.
Lovers huddle around the bonfire in the kitchen.
Funky drunks funky snore on funky couches,
someone's shoe sprouts a fern, the finches
trapped in the curtains settle into sleep.
My friend is my friend because we love
this time, when spirits expended
in a waste of shame hover near mirrors,
trying to push through, when the household gods
sit around and bitch about the quality
of their supplicants, and night terrors
grab coffee and a smoke before punching the clock.
The hour sings companionably, salty and strewn
with the corpses of pretense, broken umbrellas
on the deck of an ocean liner. We first met
here, my friend and I, and we return
whenever the pathless wood steers us
to the same clearing. Our hearts break anew
when we hear the sun sneaking through the trees
and the workaday world hard on its heels:
until next time, a toast, that it might not be our last.

Blessings From the Next New World

May the highway grab you by the face
and hoist you over the embankment
until God hangs a spoon from her nose.

May your ten thousand children each
sprout ten thousand fingers
that they might return all the library books
well before their due dates.

And may every tongue that is spoken
have a word for you, and only you,
more than just a name, more than just
another title—the sound of every voice
repeating the facts: they were here,
they were here, they were, they were.

Rust Belt Pastoral

The manhole cover at the intersection of Carver and East
went missing, now they're jacking a box truck out of the hole
with a forklift. The driver broke his teeth on the dashboard.

The Mayor watches from the diner window, animal noise
in her throat. She plucks the head off a cornflower,
crushes it, lets the petals fall on the linoleum.

In the kitchen, the cook knocks a water glass off the counter.
It shatters on the tile. The Mayor jumps, pops her umbrella
and stalks outside. The waitress sighs. Mayor didn't pay again.

Goldilocks Planet

Some people love pregnant Christian teenagers,
and some people love Thursday afternoon scalp massages,
and some people love to sweet talk their way out of quite a pickle,
but daguerreotype nudes are just right.

Some people lie badly, often, without skill,
and some people slip on the ice and don't get up,
and some people grab the barrel of the rifle pointing at them,
but licking an ice cream cone is just right.

Some people walk with God, some talk with God,
some do both, all of us do,
and most people are real as a stubbed toe:
rude, and present, and just painful enough
that it feels a little bit good,
but your face aglow in the summer afternoon sun is just right.

If Wishes Were Horses

I wish I'd spent more time as a dragonfly.
  In seventh grade, our math teacher was a mess,
sloppy, unshaven, dusted with dandruff,
  the sort of barn-sized target seventh graders
sharpen their claws on. The grapevine said
  his father was dying, and sure enough
he got a call in the middle of SOHCAHTOA,
  gave us some problems to do, and wandered off.
Chris with the bent head, his hair still parted
  in the middle, his huge nipples sticking out,
his corduroy pants hissing as he rose from his desk,
  scrawled, "Al's Dad kicks off"
on the chalkboard. No one laughed, but no one
  was brave enough to wipe the board clean.

        Al came back,
face red from crying, and he looked
  at the board, and sighed, picked up an eraser,
and started back at it, teaching us algebra,
  because what else was there to do
but share with a room of pimply ingrates
  the mysteries of trigonometry. I still hear his sigh,
usually just before I think: I wish
  I'd spent more time as a dragonfly,
hovering above a water violet, waiting to see
  if the fat mosquito I saw flitting nearby
would circle back
  so I might devour her, head first, then the rest.

After the Blizzard

The winter moon makes the snow glow
so white it's blue, as white as bone
piled on bone, until I am surrounded
not by drifts and denuded branches,
but a congregation. As we all genuflect
a strange cat melts out from an alcove
and rubs against and between my ankles.
Only then do I realize: I have no idea
how I got here, how to get home,
even what home means, but the cat knows,
and the moon knows, and that's enough.

Love, Always

Dear ____,

Tucked in a corner of the previous epistle
is a transmitter the size of a baby flea,
painted Pantone 11-0601 TCX, same color
as the envelope. It's attached with a drop
of Loctite 3189UV, the weakest point
of the apparatus, but it was all I had on hand
and really, the letter is more the point,
or it was when I started, when I was sure
words of truth and love, in blue ink
on pearly paper, would be enough to turn
your stone heart to wood, and the wood
into flame. Then I came to my senses
and added the tiny microphone, so now I know.
Boy, do I know. That you never throw away
envelopes, for one thing, that you keep them
in a drawer beside your socks, for another,
so please: now that you know that I know,
please burn said envelope, I have shoved my life
into cheap boxes and moved to a city far away
where I pray every day that you never find me.

The Beautiful Ones

Around the neighborhood we called him "Chicken,"
not because he was a coward, but because he jerked
when he walked and bobbed his head a lot, the way
a chicken does—well, more like a pigeon, but oh
that's an even worse name, especially around here,
and he was good folks, his Mamma ran the beauty store
while his Pops—really his uncle, he married
Chicken's Mamma after his Brother lost three toes
at work and died from the infection—his Pops
does makeup and lighting for some pet photographer.
Pillars of the community all, their late-summer barbecue
a sacred event from day one, and look how they brought
the Odd Fellows back from near dead, and they all sit
in the front row and stay the whole 3 hours at church,
and not just on holidays, so yeah, he's stuck with a bad
handle, but we had no choice, dude really does
walk like a chicken, even drops the occasional egg.

The Mantra (Existential My Ass)

To wake feverish in the middle of a movie
and see some actor with a face like an old rug
trying too hard, swinging from the scenery
like a marionette, is also how it feels
when death reminds us who rules,
and words that once flowed like cool water
stick in the throat, and all around people jerk
on broken sidewalks, going no place.

It's only a movie, that's the mantra,
if I keep saying it, keep moving
until words slither back into sensibility,
or at least some fishy semblance
thereof, until souls redden the faces

of the automatons again, maybe then—
then what? I'd be allowed to roll over,
bury my face in the couch's crease,
beg for strength as I dig for the remote
that I might turn the sound down
until all of creation is a distant mumble
and my hands are around its throat.

Drunk as a Prince

Dig if you will a picture
of all the lucky breaks that you missed
a tale that's told in the telling
and nobody cares that you're pissed.

The muses will whisper your fortune
what language they speak is unclear
as long as you end up in heaven
so what if you lived in arrears.

A slurry of good love and rancor
this life, a prayer made of dirt.
When doves descend they are ratlike
but they do rise like angels in church.

House Unbecoming

The wind stole the horse heads
off the wallpaper in the kitchen.
The silverware drawer flew open and howled.
The rain came through the hole in the roof
and lay on the floor with its feet in the air.
When the banister galloped out the front door
holding a box of blue tip matches in its teeth,
the chimney finally had enough: *this is the big one!*
it whooped, and the walls agreed, and the storm shutters
clapped hooray, it seemed like a real crux—
then the storm moved on, and the wind made
kissy faces in the trees, and we all settled back
into our routine, the rhapsody
of termite, sunlight, moonlight, wood rot, and echo.

Exothermia

That trees exist, appearing to stretch up
in hope of touching the sun, and of such variety:
pine, birch, ash, elm, palm, bamboo, baobab—
is proof,
    along with the grass and the rivers
and the swans and the lions and the firestorms
and fallen barns and all the silver machines,
                        of something,
what others among us might call God
but which I cannot bring myself to name,
it being as remote from my understanding
as the sun is from the topmost branch
of a leafless oak in winter, shivering but still
stretching, straining upward to embrace
    the raging wheel that gives us life.

The Caterer

In my rear view mirror, while the smoke came apart,
the pistoleros dropped their guns to sing: ¡*Ay! Sandunga,*
Sandunga mamá por Dios… but my Spanish is poor
and their mouths far away. When I returned in the evening
to gather warmers and plates and cutlery, a new scene
was already rolling, a full moon over the desert
and some burnished, waxy lips mashing together
with an intensity they hope sells well in China.

I remember the sound of their lips coming apart
as I bend to put my own lips to my daughter's head,
and I wish for her a brief puberty and an easeful
menopause, since I haven't much help to offer
with the all the nonsense in between.

R.S.V.P.

The third time they locked me in the trunk
of the achingly restored powder-blue Cadillac
I decided this was not art, comic or otherwise,
and the poignant choice of abduction spots
(in front of the abortion clinic, on a park bench
near the Hague, waiting for tickets to black midi)
did nothing to mitigate the chill of piss stains
on my trousers. So, no, Doctor VerHoovian,
I will not be attending your next installation,
nor will I continue with this graduate seminar
despite it being a requirement of my degree program,
and regardless of the status of your relationship
with my mother, which I am told balances precariously
between that of a professional wrestling tag-team
and neutron stars blinking at one another
from within distant, cloud-fuddled galaxies.

Remote Viewing Festival

The squealing tractor trailer
     shudders to a stop
just short of the crosswalk
     at the intersection
kitty-corner to my front porch.
     It is full
of fake plants: clusters of coiled ivy,
     ferns bundled
in bubble wrap, flowers piled
     atop flowers.
A squirrel on a power line
     stops to stare,
then skitters on. I'd been reading
     Pascal in the prickly
summer sun, and did not look up
     until the truck brakes
stopped their shrieking and let out
     a weary hiss.
The whole visible world is only
     an imperceptible atom
in the ample bosom of nature.
     In the silence
that follows, I can hear
    the kiss of mitochondria
joining with cytoplasm
    many billion years ago,
I can hear a fungal colony
    murmuring under my yard,
and the Rose of Sharon
    wagging in the breeze

beside my head.

       Then the truck driver

is screaming into his cell phone,

       face wine-dark

on the other side of the truck window.

       The squirrel mounts

a transformer, hops to a maple branch,

       and vanishes

into tree cover. The next sound will be

       the Earth splitting

in two, or the distant tinkling

       of an ice cream van.

It makes no difference to anyone

       which came first.

Summer Suggestion

A baby wails from a crooked row house
and I look up from my book to see
a black pickup truck, gleaming,
dripping fresh from the car wash,
cruising past the park pavilion, slowly,
then around the block, and back again,
slower. I am reading about the spread
of Neanderthals out of Europe
70,000 years ago, and the third time
the truck rolls by, I close the book
and watch: his head like a sack of rocks
with a military haircut. I'm not young
but I will do, says the lust hollowing out
his eye, says the snarled knot
at the center of his chest, the one
he keeps trying to pull apart
but only succeeds in snarling further.
The window slides further down,
I stare back. I am a good nine steps older
than he first thought. Fatter by half.
Worse, I can see all the way into him,
so he looks away, and up goes the window,
and the truck slithers on quietly,
seeming to drive itself, and without purpose—
the kind of trick that takes years of practice
under the swooping shadow of birds of prey.

Morning at the Junction

The wood is split and stacked, rose bushes
trimmed back, and it's only 9 in the morning.
The rest of the day stares back at me
from the bottom of a dried-up well.
What's next? Maybe Sudoku. Maybe a nap.
Maybe Sudoku, then a nap.
Yesterday and tomorrow are dogs on my trail.
I smell more like a goat than a goat does.

I know what it is I'm supposed to do:
look at trees. Talk to God. Find some kid
with a broken bicycle chain to fix, get to know
her hard-working single mom, let them remind me
what love is. But I know what love is.
Love is taking people to the airport.
Love is not being able to breathe at 3 am
out of worry or fear or joyful expectation.
Love is making some other soul feel that way,
which is just mean. This world is mean enough.

Like those kids across the street, leaning on cars,
smoking little electric pipes, preening
like a gaggle of Ming Dynasty courtiers.
Fewer eunuchs, maybe, clothes just as baggy,
and just as ready to kill each other
over a dirty clump of yard owned
by some Emperor they're never going to see.
Plenty enough meanness there to go around,
and that's just one corner in a world of corners.

They say you should try to leave the planet better
than you found it. I never killed anyone,
guess that makes me a success. Wood split
and stacked, roses trimmed back, sunlight
and a soft breeze, one more day spent
incorruptibly alive and wholly unnecessary.

Like the man said: wouldn't trade a hair on my head
to rule the world. A vase of roses on the mantle,
fire breathing as as the first snow falls outside,
what else? Nothing else. The point of living
is to live, and leave nothing of yourself
behind. I go to the barber once a month and listen
to failed men repeat the words of failed men
on from a TV that's bigger than the window.
I go to the bar once a week and drink 2 beers
and 1 whisky and listen to ruined children blather on
as another wall of TVs bathes them in hollow light.
I am a social animal, I need their voices
just like I need Sudoku to keep my mind
from going slack. I need Sudoku to remember
where I left my keys. I need to clip my toenails.
Yesterday and tomorrow have fallen asleep
in a bush somewhere. The clock just reached 9:30.

Statue of a Man Reading a Book

A Mama duck comes every Spring to lay eggs
in the courtyard of the High School. She always builds
her nest in the same place, between a crooked maple
and a statue of a man reading a book. The janitor
sets out water for her, and for her babies, when they come.
This year, she hatched 11, waddling the yard like bishops
while the students get ready to pass to the next grade,
or to graduate, or quit, or die. Things happen.
I confess I'm having trouble caring, about the students,
or the ducks, or even the tree. Only the statue matters.

Concrete poured into a form, I'm sure they made a thousand,
a miniature man sitting on a pedestal, clean shaven, eyes
without pupils in imitation of the unpainted Greek,
holding a slim volume titled "Truth" open in his hands.
I wonder if the faculty book club has read that one.

Like many kids, I thought statues were real bodies
posed and covered with plaster. I was wrong,
and have made of this wrongness a long habit,
it's nearly instinct, so much so that looking
out the window at ducks wandering drunk
from behind a statue, children of all sizes
peeking at them while they learn the steps
of the dance that takes us down, seems to me
a great joke played on the world, that the statue
is the only real thing in any galaxy,
a perfect scapegoat into which I can pour my sins.

In 1000 years the sun and rain will wear away

the little man and his books, or a bulldozer will turn it
under a pile of dirt and vinyl and rebar in 20,
unless someone takes pity and brings him home
to their garden. In any case, my sins,
the sins of my tribe, of all humanity,
will go with it, into the dark, formless heart of hearts
that they might be torn to pieces, devoured,
and born again. I wonder how many ducklings
will survive this season, how many
will learn to ride the curve of the earth
and find their own statues to nest behind.
Who cares. The Earth is dead. We all have died.
Every thing collapses into the one thing,
then chunders apart again, in and out and in,
wheezing like a bellows. Scapegoats, ducks, statuary:
everything I ever knew was wrong.
That is what the little man is reading in his book.

Motel Purgatorial

...no one commits suicide because life is absurd, but only because, consciously or unconsciously, life does not appear absurd enough.
—Matei Calinescu

Couples kiss goodbye on the platform
as the train wheezes, most of them praying
for a safe return, a reunion promised here
on the same platform, by the same trash can,
at the expected time, all parties involved
upright and ambulatory. A few feel discomfited,
and turn instead to furtive itineraries
or the broad, cool alleys of solitude.
Someone has written on a metal beam:
death is a terrible mistake, only a fool
would disagree. The conductor blows his whistle
and checks for stragglers, those who arrive
always alone, even when traveling together,
their bags banging against their hips as they run,
hoping this will not be the day they miss
their connection, the day all their plans
fall apart, the better life, the new love
or old friends, whatever story starts here
and ends at the station on the other end of the line,
that bet that seemed a sure thing, so sure
it wasn't enough to get them here on time.
Sometimes the conductor sees them
from the last car, tiny figures, bent and huffing
and wondering if this is it, their last chance
just pulled away with their empty seats,
and how foolish they were to believe
it could end differently, for them or anyone else.

A Gathering in Limbo

Strange days, late summer and the dogs won't stop barking
at the ghosts of dead baby skunks that haunt
the old chimney where their bones lay snuggled together
in a nest of wet ash and insulation. One night, their mother

scuttled off into the cornfield and never came home.
Her ghost hovers beside the broken down thresher,
still afraid of the ghost of the owl, still hungry
for the ghosts of frogs and voles and grubs floating

under a strange moon. We're so lucky, the dead are everywhere:
in the water we drink, the food we eat, in the air
and under the churning Earth, our cells devour the dead,
every word is a tomb built long ago on the ruins

of another. Hooray! for this wobbly orbit:
made of carrion yet fearing the dead,
eaters of lotus with nothing to forget,
to hear our own ghosts shimmering beside us,

not waiting, but telling us what it was like
to live as a thing amongst things, then no more
mewling like a calf seeking its mother, or at least,
the steaming, reeking center of any herd.

Charmed and Disarmed

We fell beneath the sheets and it seemed
like a boat had sprung a leak
so we sloshed around and bailed and bailed
until at last we surrendered, laughing,
watching it sink
in water no higher than our thighs.

I learned later she joined a cult
that preached a penitent, celibate austerity.
Not my fault, but still I'd thought
someday she would learn to navigate by starlight.

My Dwindling Sense of Possibility

At the orgy, I tripped over slippery spots
and stepped on more than one cock.
I was not invited back.

At the swinger's convention, I lost
the bag full of hotel keys.
I was not invited back.

In my first threesome, I put
all the wrong things in my mouth
and bit when I should have sucked.
I only heard about their wedding.

I tried to masturbate with my left hand
so it would feel more
like someone else.
I ended up in the hospital.

Thank God I found you, my darling.
I was about to go into politics.

The Lariat

I want to wash the hands that guide me home
and smell the soap and the soil together.

The breeze through the open window will dry us
the sun through the open window thick as butter—

I want to know salt, how it lives on the tongue,
dissolving into sensation: is that joy, or regret?

Probably both, after all, bodies are much the same,
flesh pushing against flesh until the soul

collapses like a circus tent, kisses the earth,
whispering as it falls: *someday I will lose myself*

completely. Until then, being lassoed to the world
is not so awful, as long as there are mouths to kiss,

hands to hold, flame to join with flame.

The Intermediary

Between Study Hall and Astronomy
she complains about the dairy farm
spraying manure on the fields that drain
into the creek running beside her house.

Between Astronomy and the long drive home
she texts her son to get him out of bed
and on to work. If he loses this job
he'll be out on his ass, this time for real.

Between loading the dishwasher and folding
the laundry, her mother calls, her sister calls,
and the cat shits on the kitchen floor.
Her husband tells her about the cat shit.

After everyone is asleep, she sits
and smokes cigarettes on the dark porch,
wondering what it would be like to get cancer
or win the lottery, and what's the difference.

She drops a butt into a coffee can
as a doe melts free from the trees and stands
staring, eyes black and endless as space.
She feels her body falling toward them,

into the formlessness that birthed stars —
she rattles the screen, hisses "shoo!",
but the deer does not move, does not move,
then lifts an ear and dissolves back into trees.

She lights another, spits, puts it out,
stares into the gaps between pine and oak,
wondering how many eyes stare back,
how much of the world they could swallow.

Oh, That Wasn't There Before, He Said

When first I learned the world was round,
a goddamn ball, I was dubious, and snot-nosed.
Next night I dreamed I was a train

carrying a spool of track with me, laying it
down across the steppe as I went,
between mountains, looping bridges

from island to island, pulling the rails
and ties up behind me as I rolled.
I gathered maps, love letters from explorers

born the minute they stood upright and saw
all there was to see on that side of the world,
above the couch, across the veldt.

Piles of maps, a mountain of everywhere:
Brno, Darwin, Lagos, Bangkok, Tripoli, Chicago,
the Danube, the Yangtze, Victoria Falls.

Then the world started to shrink, squealing,
hull timbers giving way in a wreck of a storm,
chundering sea and wave: work and death

and obligation, every tomorrow maunders,
drives me back to the dull harbor. I know
that brick. That traffic cone. Kitchen funk.

I know what pettiness to expect of my neighbors
and what of the same they should expect from me.

I know the sermon as I know the preacher's teeth.

The train whistle only makes me check my watch.
I stopped at the mirror yesterday morning
and saw in my face a map to nowhere:

empty valleys, bald mountains, cracked rivers,
an old man up all night on a cold train station bench
waiting to hear the whistle blow from inside.

Syllogistically Yours

This world has a terrible haircut
and it groans getting out of the car,
therefore, God is a soliloquy
discussing winter's enjambment of autumn.

This world is a box of crayons left on a radiator
and it walks like a duck and talks like a duck,
therefore, God is the smell of oatmeal with butter
after a night dancing in puddles of pink champagne.

This world is a mound of used kleenex
nested atop a gleaming, polished rat's skull,
therefore, God has fallen asleep
at a booth in the back of the diner.

Not even a kiss from a defibrillator will wake her.

When Love Endures Like a Clock Painting Itself

When I was just a baby, all I wanted to do
was get fucked up, make some art,
chase girls. Now, older, getting towards dead,
all I want to do is get fucked up,
make some art, I caught a girl. She caught me.

America is America's worst nightmare.
Individual words are for sale: God,
for example, is a greasy flea market find.
I caught a girl, she understands. We chew
America's entrails lightly, as not to choke.

My phone is a baby phone, all it wants to do
is play Big 2 and squirt notifications at me.
I bought the phone, indentured servants
somewhere in Tianjin made it. I am developing
an app to measure my guilt, and order pills.

Another friend killed themselves last night,
so we went out and had steak. It's only right,
thick, fat-basted chunks of charred flesh
in my mouth. I only wish I could spit some
into his dead mouth like a mama bird.

All these tasks, ribbons to cut and alms to beg,
all these things that keep us from loving the world
and each other, but must be done. Or not,
I haven't the strength to find out, all I want to do
is find where love has broken through the pavement.

If my brain comes apart, push me in a shopping cart
down the expressway to the countryside.
Leave me with the corn and the cows.
Get me away from the crackling wireless, let me
flit like a moth, let the modern world go on alone.

The mushrooms that grew beside the garage
were delicious. All those dreams where they found
the corpse I buried in the yard, that was fungi
sending me messages from home, care packages.
I want to eat mushrooms that sprout from my skin.

Dreams in the board room, in towers of black glass:
target the accused with micro-ads while they wait
for the judge algorithm to text their sentence.
Just following some rule: be fruitful and metastasize,
or, what's gone is gone, or, let there be light.

I watched a drone hover above a garbage scow
plodding downriver, sun at its back.
Two old men pointed their fishing poles at it,
shook their heads, cracked fresh cans of beer.
Don't remember what happened the rest of the year.

There, again, the thought that I've yet to wake
from a drowning sleep, that I will open my eyes
and my throat and all the world will rush in.
There is no remedy for this world, and no better
place to drift, at least, none that I've found.

She leaves little piles of mail everywhere
the way bunnies leaves turds behind them,

a crooked trail of circulars, credit card offers,
the Publishers' Clearing House, I gather them up
and use them to start the fireplace roaring.

Domestication is mastication, the making of pap.
Also compost, also slurry, also a souffle.
The evening cocktail, the bed that gathers us up
in its soft hands. If my brain comes apart,
nestle me within the scent of that girl I caught.

Like a fledgling abandoned on a moonless night
like a hammer whose handle has rotted away
like unsettled laughter heard round a corner
like the last flutters of the last film reel being played
love unattended grows faceless and gray.

I love watching her wash her hair in the sink.
Not sure why it excites me, except it makes me think
what a mystery it is to love another, what a divine
and impossible wonder, words whispered
through the walls, from one cave to another.

East Jesus and Why I Never Made It There

While drinking in the rain with my friend Charlie
he laughed about the girl that dyed herself
blue, how she touched the wall and said
she could feel all the people that ever touched it,
all the people that built it. I pointed out
he'd done the same thing in the alley
behind the punk rock bar, touched a wall
and channeled the spirits. *Oh yeah*, he said.

Charlie died on a recliner on a slab in the desert
not enough years ago. I expect many an ass
has sat in that chair since, just the way Charlie
sits in our heads every so often.

Drunk in the rain, we sang all the way through
Springsteen's *Nebraska* album,
having figured out we both knew all the words.
We whooped the last chorus of "Reason to Believe"
and the rain stopped. It was cinematic,
the same way all shadows are, the same way
we leave tatters of spirit in the walls we touch.

Things Ain't What They Used to Be Again

These new neighbor kids
are apocalyptic little doves,
bicycle-bound destroyers of worlds,
chambermaids to the ice cream inquisitor,
torturers of legendary proportion
in the lore of neighborhood squirrels.
We are not squirrels, and so must follow
the rule: *save the children,*
save the babies, like Marvin Gaye sang.
Marvin's father, Marvin Senior,
shot Marvin Junior with the .38
his son had given him for Christmas.
Reverend Gay always swore: if any
of my children should strike me,
I will murder them, and thus kept
his promise. 2000 generations ago
our ancestors started behaving
the way we behave, making fire
and art and knives that would butcher
or murder or announce their bearer's
status. The tallest neighbor boy
just turned a chipmunk's head to pulp
with a golf club. Mercy, mercy me.

Gallus Gallus

Thought I'd left the chickens
back on the farm
but the furry brown clump that fell off
those old boots I pulled out
the back of the closet
smells unmistakeably of shit and feathers.

I opened the window meaning to toss
the chip of sod out into the alley,
where black windows
dead-eyed stare down
at trash and air conditioning units,
and put it instead in a box
with my Boy Scout badges
and the Tom T. Hall cassette
Dad played in his truck
over and over and over again.

image: Bill E. Evans

Maybe Next Time

At the table where the hostess put
the people who just didn't fit
with anyone else, I put down the bottle
and watched them dance.
We all did, and we all thought
the same two thoughts:
I want to have a love like that, and
why don't I have a love like that.

Once they finished, and the song
changed, and the children
came out to hop around the floor,
we peeked at each other sideways,
trying to gauge which misfit here
might someday dip me in my silk dress,
or which would let me dip her,
which would trust me not to drop her,
which would think it a great joy
to be held just above the ground
by someone with the power to let go.

image: Bill E. Evans

Depot, Junction, Terminus

Everyone who's lived beside train tracks
has taken it into their mind to jump aboard,
to strap tomorrow to the whistle
and blow on down the track.

Almost no one, these days, has done more
than take it into their mind. These days,
be likely to get an arm torn off, the trains
go faster than our dreams allow.

Instead, most end up station masters,
out on the platform with the sign saying:
pass on by, no reason to stop here,
hoping the conducter sees, and waves.

image: Bill E. Evans

Family Photo Time

Two men and a woman, scowling,
pull garbage and nearly garbage
from the dead man's garage.

A voice directs me to catalog the pile,
that he lived, died, how stuffs and things
also dead or dying, are strewn at the curb.

Not a bad fate. I'd happily leave this body
at curbside, there's some metal in my ankle,
in my jaw, not worth a scrapper's time.

The constituent elements of a human body
are worth $4.50, I've read, the skin
more than the rest. Extraction is the nut.

It's like leaning into a blizzard, trying to resist
the bodies' urge to go back
to what is was, a gold coin that wishes

to return to the mountain. But we cannot
go back, not really, can only go on,
head down, eyes pinched against the blizzard,

hoping what gets left at the curb
is worth a glance from a passerby
before the truck comes and hauls it away.

New Boss, Old Boss

Each burning boat in Caesar's rear,
* Flames—No return through me!*
                    —Melville

Got those Roman legionary blues,
as though the ship that brought me here
turns to cinders at my back
and the man who gave the order
is less a god and more a goon
but we follow him regardless
toward death and night and blood
since there's nowhere else to go
and to survive, we must murder
because the goon, that craven shit,
wants all the songs to be about him
but he's just a husk without us,
who cares what lies the singers sing.

I feel that way on deadlocked days
when all the goons with all the cash
are whining how it's just too hard
to stay so rich they'll never die,
and the singers vie to lick goon ass
until their mouths are yawning sores
and no one prays but bows and scrapes
'cause heaven and hell keep bickering:
whose turn is it to watch the kids?
There is no wealth, no other world,
without our sweat and hopelessness
and yes, we could just wander off

49

into the woods, some foreign land,
away from burning ships, from steel
that flashes in our hands,
but few are rough enough to spite
the hand that holds the next day's wage,
the morsels for the mewling babes,
a chance to lick the greasy plates
while the rats watch and wait their turn.
Imagining a righteous wind
some distant day might blow
seems a paltry hope to hinge
any kind of life upon.

So death to dreams, and search instead
for a place among the crannies,
for once the unbeholden songs
are joined, dance will follow.
Those of us who chose instead
to render unto Caesar
will die the same way all must die,
but some of us might come instead
to live as melody.

Pedagogy

The slouching cheerleader dangles
her mother's Birkenstock
from the end of her foot.

Boredom is a sign of defeat,
Coach says. Coach would know,
she smells like the pink wine

she sucks out of the sports bottle
she keeps in the cup holder
of her PT cruiser, and goes out

into the hallway 6 times a day
to text her ex-husband.
What does she know about

victory, what does she know
about watching a sister
shrivel up and blow away

in an oxygen tent, or a father
who needs a fistful of pills
just to keep the voices at bay.

Or maybe she does. The sandal
falls, clatters on the gym floor,
Coach's knife face swings out

then softens, watching the girl try

to scoop it up and slip it on
without anyone noticing,

her hands shaking like branches
in the wind that comes over the lake.

Migrations Large and Small

On legs so skinny they seem about to snap
she speed-hobbles her way across the parking lot
to the cabinet factory and ten hours of studying
laminate for imperfections, a small bag of cocaine
waiting for her at the end, in the false bottom
of her jewelry box. Her mother drives the two blocks
to Seven Eleven in a cloud of Jesus and Estée Lauder,
buys three air fresheners and a bottle of sweet tea
from the cashier who limps around behind the register
on his new prosthesis, emblazoned with
the American Flag, an eagle, crossed carbines—
his stump is sore and chapped and his wife
might rub some Eucerin on it when he gets home,
if she's not too tired, or too disgusted,
as she loves but cannot bear to touch
the place where the IED snapped off a part of him.
She tells the Pastor how it makes her skin crawl,
touching the folds, the lumps, and he puts his hand
on her shoulder and says, "why do angels need legs?"
She thinks he means well. She stares
at the chipped polish on the toes sticking out
the front of her sandals, and wonders how it came to be
that people could wander the whole of the earth
in a few generations, and still never find
a valley where love might flourish sure as wheat,
a place we could stop, and sit, and just watch it grow.

Monday Morning Team Call

Ok people, today is the day
my head explodes, viscera on the walls,
the whole deal. Charlie! What do you think?
Mohan! Becky! Let's center ourselves.
I hear it, I hear the question
you all want to ask but won't: why?
Why would your head explode?
It's just a figure of speech, but, still,
why? Because we have a job to do,
no, a calling, no, we have a world
rubbing against us like a cat,
and just like a cat, it could walk away
at any point, poof! Under a hedge,
or a bed, no more leg rubbing,
no more whiskers. We need to get sharp,
laser-focused, but dense as a cloud
and agile as a silkworm. Brian!
Time to get all Cirque du Soleil
on their asses, all batshit lordy lordy,
right Raheem? With me Monash?
Let's get right up in their grills and let it fly,
if we don't, we die. As a concern, I mean.
As a gifter of steaks and cigars
and wellness certification. No more of that,
Anna Banana, no more cushy ergonomics
or spray pens with wifi, back to the room
with a table, a chair, a cactus, a window
that looks out on the parking lot,
the bad side where no one parks
because the shredder and dumpster

live there, waiting for a car to eat.
Bob! Good job on the lunch meat projections.
Tara! Management said your monthly
was synchronized, a few more like that
and we'll all be sending you our nail
and hair clippings. This is it, people,
the day we go over the top and see
all the abandoned machine gun nests,
all the gutted nomenclature, all the spent
world in all its spent glory. First round
is on me, Applebee's, 6 pm, no public fisting
this time, hey Bernice! Second round
on me too, all the rounds on me if we hit
this number right here ( ) that's our goal,
nail that puppy and the whole aquarium
is on me, what do I care, my head
will be splattered all over my monitors,
Loretta, can you quick put in a call
to HR, make sure my loved ones
all get an eye or tooth? Just kidding,
I have no loved ones, nobody does,
so let's do this. Let's do it three hundred times,
let's do it 'til our urethras all flip
inside out spontaneously, until our parents
call to ask how we're doing, until the dogs
come marching home to demand
their names back, and no more naked dancing
in the kitchen or I will bite you. Ok. Questions?

Inside Normal

Work is the single most demeaning thing
most people do every day.

Not working is even more demeaning,
but less common.

This is why we are told to find a passion.
If you have the bad luck

of your passion and your work coinciding,
the shit you are in is bottomless,

especially if this work involves other people,
as work inevitably does.

Work is so demeaning that we celebrate
when we no longer notice.

Realizing the value of our hours, our bodies,
and how much is wasted on work

would drive most of us out of the pasture
and into the pond

with rocks in our pockets and the sky
in our eyes.

The Hole Where My Tooth Used To Be

After I die, if I die, who will play me
in the movie about my life?
A brine shrimp, maybe, or a distended
grizzly bear's asshole. The part
of my first kiss should be played
by a stick of unsalted butter,
and the whole shebang should be shot
in an abandoned gelateria
by a rooster with a GoPro on its head.
Here is the speech my surrogate can read
when the picture wins ten thousand Oscars:
Big Dummies of the world! You are not alone!
We can be any dream, slap any river,
once we put fear in a headlock
and make snow angels in the summer dew.
I'd like to thank everyone who died
before I did, especially Dr. Jonas Salk
and the Divine Wives of Amun,
and I wouldn't be here if my parents
had not fornicated, so, hooray for orgasms!
I would prefer the actual statuary
be melted down and used in the production
of space telescopes, but I'll be dead,
so whatever, everyone will just keep on
doing what they were doing.

Attending the Conference

Wake and ruminate on the cud of tyranny!
Such was the offer, and a small honorarium
besides, how could I refuse? An hour's drive
through winter swamps, cardboard cups
of weak coffee, a little powerpoint foreplay
and we're off: who murdered your dreams,
little man? Or did you simply slip and fall
and impale yourself on data points 1 – 92.2?
And you, daughter of Herodias, do you weep
when your parking pass is not validated?
A few more turns of the screw, then it's time
for boxed lunch. I burrow out and escape
to the gas station, eat cheese in my car.
Maybe if I wore old-style aviator goggles
on my head, the Human Resources Department
would ignore me. *Year-end goal one:*
eat less cheese at the gas station. Goal two:
sing more to plants of all sizes. Goal three:
liberation from Samsāra. No, I am not
taking this seriously, because I have negotiated
with each of my selves, and have reached
consensus: we must persist. Everything else
is just another subordinate clause, another
ring tone, another diamond saw, another
butcherbird, another easterly squall.
I have collected enough sick days to slay
three tiny Caesars, and even if that is not
what sick days are for, well, they keep me
from splashing across the Rubicon, skull throbbing
with the disease that turns men into kings.

Just Stay In Bed (In Your Mind)

Woke up on the wrong side of my head,
the slushy part, the side all the bad ideas
run across like ball bearings on the deck
of a listing barge. Everything clatters,
the oatmeal, the broom, the cat, seems I'm alive
inside a shivering mouth, teeth chattering,
lips a-quiver, spit me out! But don't, please,
must be colder down there on the sidewalk
waiting for the rain to pull me into the flume,
gutter to river, river to sea. I'll stay here, thanks,
among the shattered angels of my better nature,
and I'll read once more the book that explains
how the difference between myself and plankton
is mostly in my head, and surely on
the wrong side, the slushy part, and yes,
I will do better next time, I will be credulous,
I will believe, or least perform
something resembling that affliction.

Seven Day Tribe

The congregation, swollen with wine,
spurts out onto the sidewalk
muttering *te deums*, spoiling for a fight.

They dock at the donut shop.
Cooler heads. Sugared belly-warmth.
Who made the sabbath the sabbath,
after all! Dexterous at the game
of prayer, mantis hands sawing
through crullers and bears claws,
blessed by every measure, dissolving,
once the feast is depleted,
back into couples, trios, families,
hard-nosed singletons, all reeling
along the sidewalk in the afternoon sun.

In six days, the string will tauten
and all will return, surely as the universe
collapsing back in on itself, then bursting
again. The donut maker is happy,
but everyone else is just making do
with threadbare stories of sacrifice
from a time when blood meant blood.
The donut maker was happy then, too.

What's For Dinner?

As I walk to my car I step over rabbit prints
in the fresh snow. Each set is a little cluster,
back and front feet together, as though the hare
sat here, then there, then further on,
levitating from spot to spot. I imagine
rabbit eyes peeking at me from under a hedge.

The forecasters announced a bitter cold
tonight, but I trust the bunny to hunker
properly and make it through, unlike people,
who die all manner of foolish ways
on nights as cold as what's expected.
I trust human malformity as much
as I trust rabbits to be tasty, jugged or braised,
as much as I trust bacteria to eat their bones,
my bones, the whole boneyard we shiver in.

Those Were The Days, My Friend

I remember when we first became
        computers,
back in the Pleistocene, hurtling over
        the tundra,
hooking our talons around the wheel
        of a Trans Am,
chugging codeine and kombucha
        out of a broken
ostrich skull. Didn't last long, nothing
        does, not
the uncanny valley, not the horsehair
        worm,
not *My Beautiful Laundrette*, not
        the pole star.
Nothing is still. Even God wears
        a saddle.
Especially God. Before we became
        computers,
we were slow enough to remember
        the way
to the moon and stars. Now we just
        fling each other
and lick at our bleeding hands and feet
        and keep pretending
that once up on a time we were
        creatures of sense.

I'll Make You Forget the Rest

The Milky Way remains unimpressed
by my successful production of iambs and such.
I search for my face in the late night sky —
my last song rattled like a skull full of nails,
enough, I thought, for some minor constellation
to take notice. Instead, I am a vampire staring into
a broken mirror, shaking a bouquet of yellowed sonnets
at the room I would swear I am standing in,
though my eyes tell me otherwise.
The only worse fate I can imagine:
the Milky Way suddenly taking notice.

Gathering of Stones

A lone oak in a stubbly corn field ,
throbs in late-winter wind. Someone
has built for it an audience of stones,
stood on their ends, fat part in the dirt,
skinny part in the air, just like people.
The lousy poets among them have sagged,
lain down and surrendered to chatter:
broken race cars, intergalactic pandemics,
5k charity sorties into the heart of Africa.
They have my sympathy. We all fall down.
But while there is only one heaven,
more hells exist than there are souls
to fill them, and we have some choice
in the matter, never mind what oak branches
seem to whisper—or is that just the wind
talking, telling the tree a shaggy story
about all the forests it has blown through,
and no one ever stacked the stones at all.

Living Large, Thinking Small

Nothing concerns me: not death,
not injustice, not my craven people,
not my craven self. Nothing
is my blessing, a lotus
enfolding and unfolding, trees bursting
with ripe fruit. When the wheel of Samsāra
comes rolling along, I flatten myself
to the ground, and the ground consents
to give way beneath me. While the world
burns, I sleep, like cool rain
drifting through the smoke's shadow.

I neither radiate nor absorb,
I eat when spoken to, I speak
whatever is put on my plate.
I am everywhere and alone.
That swan sailing by in the fog knows me.
That ceramic dog on the table calls me
by name. A clock ticks, one second
to the next, and a gear inside me slips.
I collapse like a building, and all the stars
stare down coldly at my ruin.
Moored to the mute earth,
I am only here, now, and alone
waiting for the clock to tick one more time.

Budapest Corners

What soft hands she must have had, the mother
of all the children who questioned the revolution.

What soft hands burped the ones who later swore
allegiance to a blood truth
and live now as statues in the shade beside a pond.

She must have called them names as sugar-sweet
as the names in the hotel vending machine.

Not So Fragile Really

If we weren't fighting, we were fucking,
nothing in between but laundry.
An old, stupid story:
this is how families get made.

We wandered, dazed as crash victims.
The only ones who knew
what was really going on
were the microbes in our underwear.

One night I wriggled down
to bury my tongue in her labia
and my left calf muscle seized
so I yelped and rolled away.

We never fought or fucked again.
The thing about making love is:
it's better than masturbation
but it takes so much more work.

Mobilization

Trouble sounds its crooked bell
and we march toward it, hands out
as though walking in the dark
because we are walking in the dark,
bodies breathing beside our bodies,
each drawn forward by the tolling
in the distance, each marching forward
for the sake of the bodies that march
beside them, for the rhythm of their steps.

The sound swells, echoes, swells again,
and one-by-one, bodies start to glow
and oh! Thy neighbor's face emerges,
and oh! Thine own, gazing back.
The darkness, hoisted on this light
beggars into the sky, moans between stars,
and the song of doves and birch begins,
and the song of lovers' whispers,
and the drifting marigold, and the murmur
of jasmine, and honeysuckle, and phlox,
and the first gentle laugh rings out
and no longer are we marching, but dancing
and eating and making love in hay bales,
deaf, for a time, to the crooked bells
tolling from the other side of the mountains,
from deep in the earth, from above the sky.

We All Will Make the Little Flowers Grow

The alarm blazes in my chest: time's up!
All the curling yellow leaves, the oceans
of yellow leaves pushing across the yard,
around the bare trees, into the street,
under the wheels of the cars hissing by,
sticking to the soles of shoes and so delivered
to the bank floor, the court house floor,
to kitchens and mud rooms across the city,
down interstates to a hundred other cities,
up the gangplank to the decks of cargo ships,
fluttering down onto containers full
of wheat, or motherboards, or dolls,
blown free as the crane swings over the wharf—
time's up! I'll never see the yellow leaves again,
the alarm has sprung, so: no more words,
no more the taste of words in my mouth,
no more the tarantella of words along the page,
no more the fortress of books around me,
no more the walk to and from the library,
yellow leaves coiling around my ankles—
no more, once the alarm sounds,
because then, at last, I wake.

The Dismantling of Christ the King Preparatory Academy

Bricks formed by the sins of the father
bricks fired in the sins of the mother
mean nothing to the hazmat suits,
to their clicking fists, the twitching readout.

The ghosts of priests hover anxious, cherubs,
the ghosts of nuns imagine their heads banging on the floor
as the casements are pried from the windows
and the blackboards clatter on the green tile.

The Apostle's Creed was learned on that bench,
Tennyson from that lectern, those bunsen burners—
the dumpster is full and in a restricted area.
They dismantle it all like an instance of thrombosis.

Late Night Movie Marathon

Brains, brains! Zombified
spooge in a bone chalice,
soft wet throne of self—
brains! Who eats and who
gets eaten, what thinks and what
gets thunk. Buddha brain,
lizard brain, paleo-snark
from the top of the meat tree,
pre-frontal lobotomy or
the bottle in front of thee?
Brain drain, brain storms,
blues eyes crying in my
brain brain brain, yes
it hurts a lot. We always do.
Where the flavor comes from,
where the slink resides
when the body is not
actively slinking. Brains!
Our love, our negation, monstrous
and that which slays
the monster, all snug together,
all raging to leave the nest.
Sweets for my sweet,
brains for my brains,
I have fed and feed
and always the hunger, still.

The Chattering Place

The bird that spoke to me Sunday morning
hated hawks. *Always lurking, bad neighbors,*
once a hawk moves in, life is fear.

But, red of tooth and claw, right?
Blake was a twat. Blake never flew.
The morning too lovely to argue,

then the stones in the garden wall started
their complaint: *too cold*
too hot too cold too crowded free us, dear sir.

Bah, soon enough the sky will be yours!
But they just moan, and the trees goad them until
my lovely morning explodes with chatter.

So, I head to the basement to listen to the worms,
all mad gamblers, laying odds left and right
on the circumambulations of grubs and mites,

20 on Pepito! 40 on Little Ed! They convene
between roots, ready for a little entertainment
after a hard day sucking through loam.

The fungus is singing like a chorus of monks.
The spiders shout back and forth, arguing
arcane turns of arachnid philosophy.

There is nothing left to do but lay on the floor,
which says only the same thing again and again:
I am not a floor. I am the roof of a room you cannot see.

Running Errands in The Drowned City

It's hard to see someone so addled, so early in the morning.
Bright pink hair, pacing the parking lot like a wind-up toy,
screaming at a cell phone held as far away as her arms allow.

The pharmacy is thronged as soon as it opens. Five strollers,
a line at the take-your-own-blood-pressure machine.
The pharmacist chews her lip in the glow of her computer.

Here, an accidental mouth speaks truth to power,
over there, an intentional mouth, meatily slapping—
so many mouths, bouquets of lips and teeth and tongue.

Back outside, a baby's shoe, upside down atop a sewer grate.
I nudge it upright with my own gigantic shoe:
muddy, patches of ruby sparkles still shining through.

The grocery doors swing halfway, pause, then slide
fully open. I pass through, followed by my grandmother's ghost.
I stand beside a mound of oranges, baffled.

The woman shoves a package of steaks under her thigh,
pushes the lever "forward" on her electric wheelchair.
The stock boy and I exchange a glance, a shrug,

I check another item off my to-do list.

In the Parking Lot of a Hardware Store (Never)

It's finally hot outside. Spring was, again, negligible, so
I'm sitting here in the steam after getting a few two by fours,
and the longest nails they had, and some paint samples.
The front porch needs about a hundred coats, something purple:
we're inching our way toward inhabiting an art compound,
though nothing so elaborate as East Jesus. At least, not yet.
Here are some of the shades of purple you missed: *Sovereign*,
Muscat Grape, Evening Slipper, King's Court. Unimaginable.
I like Mata Hari best, as our porch is a spy's perch
overlooking a slow, but busy, intersection. My neighbor says
when the law changed to right-on-red, there was an accident
every day for a month. Once the paint dries,
I'll imagine you all sitting there beside me, spying
on passers-by, waiting for an accident, laughing
because I'd done something as stupid, as human,
as imagining the dead into existence. Then, I'll go in the basement
and crucify a TV set to the two by fours and plant it
in the front yard, to scare away—not crows, not deer,
but something else, the same thing we all fought against
and hid from, and I'll say, *see, that is why we were friends, now
you can go*. But you won't go, and that's another reason
we were friends. There is no end to the love that blinds us.

Saying Grace at the Beggar's Banquet

My friends, my enemies,
those I have not met:
I ask you to join me in a song
celebrating the latest
orbital anniversary
I have stumbled upon,
wherein I look at photographs
of my wedding
and recognize those who have died
in nearly every frame.

I ask you to sing
and celebrate a day,
like all days, worthy
of the fullest praise
if only because
I still have the means
to sing, and to beg you
do the same,
for the same reason.

Pski's Porch Publishing was formed July 2012, to make books for people who like people who like books. We hope we have some small successes.

Pski's Porch

323 East Avenue
Lockport, NY 14094
www.pskisporch.com

www.ingramcontent.com/pod-product-compliance
Lightning Source LLC
Chambersburg PA
CBHW071238090426
42736CB00014B/3129

* 9 7 8 1 9 4 8 9 2 0 2 5 4 *